TELL ME WHY the Earth is like a jigsaw

Barbara Taylor

KINGFISHER

KINGFISHER

First published 2013 by Kingfisher
an imprint of Macmillan Children's Books
a division of Macmillan Publishers Limited
20 New Wharf Road, London N1 9RR
Basingstoke and Oxford
Associated companies throughout the world
www.panmacmillan.com

Concept by Ray Bryant
Designed and illustrated by Dynamo Design

ISBN 978-0-7534-3681-3

Copyright © Macmillan Publishers Ltd 2013

2 4 6 8 9 7 5 3 1
1TR/0413/WKT/UG/128MA

A CIP catalogue record for this book is available from the British Library.

Printed in China

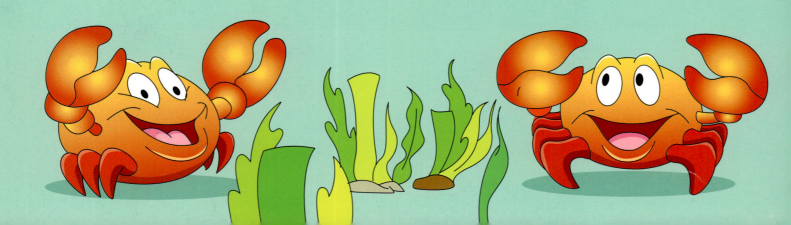

Contents

Tell me why...

the Earth needs a blanket

The thin blanket of gases around the Earth shields it from the Sun's harmful rays and from meteors. It also stops the Earth from getting too hot or too cold. This blanket is called the atmosphere, and life on Earth could not exist without it. Living things need to breathe the air in the atmosphere to stay alive. The atmosphere becomes thinner (contains less air) further away from the Earth, which is why it is hard for climbers to breathe high up on mountains.

If you could look at the Earth from a spaceship, you would see the atmosphere as a thin, blue haze around the planet.

Uncovered Moon

The Moon does not have an atmosphere because the pulling force of its gravity is too weak to hold any gases around it. The Earth's gravity is much stronger, and so holds its blanket of gases in place.

5

Tell me why...
it gets dark at night

The Earth is a spinning ball of rock that takes one day and one night (24 hours) to turn around once. When your part of the Earth turns away from the Sun, the Sun's light cannot reach you, so it gets dark. This is when you have night-time. When your part of the Earth turns around to face the Sun again, sunlight can reach you once more, so you have daytime. While you are having breakfast, people on the other side of the Earth are going to sleep!

Surprising Sun

The Sun seems to rise in the sky during the day and sink down again at night, but it is actually the movement of the Earth that causes this. As the Earth spins around, it makes the Sun appear to rise and set.

In places near the north and south poles, the Sun stays low in the sky at night for six months of the year. So, for half the year it is light at night there.

Tell me why...
some places have four seasons

The four seasons of spring, summer, autumn and winter are regular changes in the pattern of the weather. These seasons happen because the Earth is tilted at an angle as it moves around the Sun. In spring and summer the Earth is tilted towards the Sun, so the weather is warmer, with long, bright days. In autumn and winter the Earth is tilted away from the Sun, so the weather is colder, with shorter days and long, dark nights.

Hibernation

Some animals, such as marmots and bats, survive the long, cold winter months by retreating into their cave or burrow and going into a very deep sleep. This is called hibernation.

Animals that hibernate, such as this dormouse, eat a lot in autumn and use stored body fat to stay alive during their winter sleep.

Tell me why...
the Earth has a cold top and bottom

The polar lands at the top and bottom of the Earth are cold because the Earth's surface is curved. The Sun's rays have to travel further through the Earth's atmosphere to reach these lands, and they are weaker when they arrive. The rays are also spread out over the Earth's curved surface, which reduces their heating power. All the white ice and snow in polar lands makes them even colder. This is because the white colour reflects most of the Sun's rays, so the heat bounces back into the sky.

Hot waist
Around the middle of the Earth – its 'waist' – the Sun's rays hit the planet full on and its heat is concentrated, making it very hot in this region. The green plants that grow there reflect only 20 per cent of the Sun's heat.

Many kinds of penguin live in the cold lands at the bottom of the Earth. Often, penguins huddle together in big groups to share warmth, taking it in turns to stand in the middle.

Tell me why...
some mountains breathe fire

Red-hot, liquid rock from deep inside the Earth sometimes bursts through cracks in the surface to produce fountains of fire. This helps to cool the centre of the Earth, which is incredibly hot. On the surface, the liquid rock cools down into solid rock and forms mountains called volcanoes. The red-hot rock may be pushed up to the surface by bubbles of gas. The bubbles in a bottle of fizzy drink can make the liquid spray out of the top of the bottle in a similar way.

The hot rock that explodes out of a volcano can be ten times hotter than boiling water! It slides along at speeds of up to 180 metres per second.

Hot baths

Hot rock sometimes heats up underground water, which rises to the surface to form bubbling hot springs. In the mountains of Japan, macaque monkeys often take baths in hot springs to keep warm in the winter.

11

Tell me why...
the Earth is like a jigsaw

The surface of the Earth is like a giant jigsaw puzzle because it is made up of pieces, called plates, that fit together. There are about 14 large plates and 38 smaller ones. Most plates contain some of the Earth's continents (big areas of land) and some of the ocean floor. Hot rocks churning around inside the Earth make the plates slip and slide about. This makes the continents move around, so they are in different places today than they were millions of years ago.

Creeping continents

The way continents move about on the surface of the Earth is known as continental drift. They drift only a few centimetres each year though, which is about the same speed as your fingernails grow.

The Himalayas formed when the plate carrying India pushed into the one carrying the rest of Asia. The rocks in between the two plates were pushed up to make mountains.

12

Tell me why...
the Earth shakes and cracks open

When energy stored in underground rocks is suddenly released at a weak point in Earth's surface, an earthquake happens, making the ground tremble and shake. Sometimes the surface splits apart along a jagged line called a fault, as huge blocks of rock slide past each other or move up or down. The biggest earthquakes are caused by plate movements and can destroy buildings and bridges. In some areas, where earthquakes happen a lot, buildings are built to be 'earthquake proof'. They are flexible and have strong foundations, so they do not crumble when the ground shakes.

Giant waves

If an earthquake happens under the sea, it can trigger a giant wave called a tsunami (soo-naam-ee). Tsunamis can travel at speeds of up to 800 kilometres per hour and reach heights of about 30 metres near the coast.

Many buildings were destroyed in the big San Francisco earthquake of 1989, in the USA, which lasted only 10–15 seconds. It was caused by rocks sliding past each other along the San Andreas fault line.

13

Tell me why...

there are chimneys in the ocean

Super-hot seawater, heated by volcanic rock deep within the Earth's crust, can spout out of cracks called vents in the ocean bed. The super-heated water contains lots of minerals, which drop out in the cold seawater on the ocean floor. The minerals stick together and build up to form tall chimneys. As the hot water flows up through the chimneys, it turns the water black or white, making them look like real chimneys with smoke pouring out of the top!

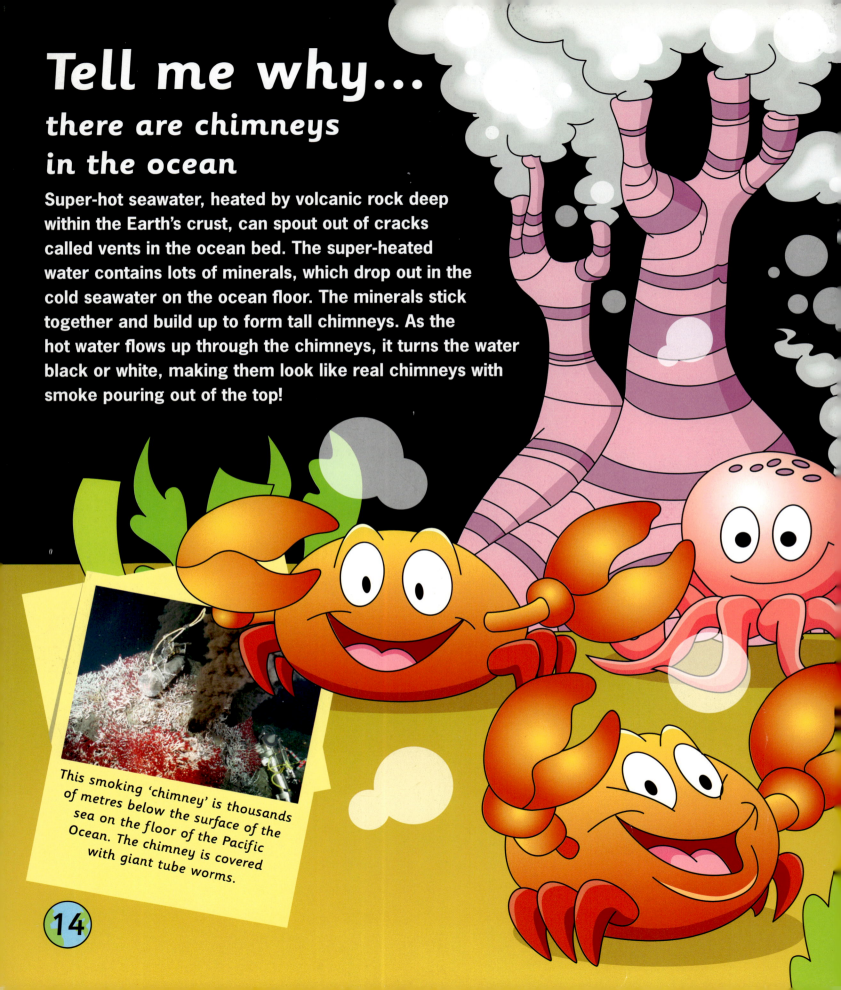

This smoking 'chimney' is thousands of metres below the surface of the sea on the floor of the Pacific Ocean. The chimney is covered with giant tube worms.

14

Creatures of the deep

Unusual creatures live in the dark around the chimneys. There are giant tube worms one-metre long, blind shrimps, sea snails, octopuses and giant clams as big as dinner plates!

15

Tell me why...
rain falls from the sky

The rain that falls from the sky starts off as water on the ground. The Sun heats the water, turning it into an invisible gas called water vapour. The water vapour rises up into the sky, where it cools down and turns back into tiny drops of water again. Billions of water drops collect together to form clouds, which float in the sky. When the clouds are heavy enough, the water drops fall down to the ground as rain. Rain clouds often look grey because they are so full of water that light can't shine through them.

Cloud shapes

Clouds come in different shapes and sizes. Wispy ice clouds float high in the sky. Fluffy cumulus clouds look like cotton wool, but can grow into giant, thunderstorm clouds. Flat stratus clouds cover the sky in a grey duvet.

These are storm clouds gathering over the city of Kiev, in the Ukraine. They are called cumulonimbus clouds – cumulus means 'heap' and nimbus means 'cloud'.

16

Tell me why...
rainbows are so colourful

Rainbows show us the colours in sunlight that are usually hidden from our eyes. As light shines through raindrops, the water makes the colours spread out so that we can see each one by itself. From the ground, a rainbow is shaped like an arch, but if you look down from a plane, it is possible to see a circular rainbow! We all see a slightly different rainbow because of the way the sunlight bounces off the raindrops into our eyes.

Moonbow

If the Moon shines brightly through the rain, it may create a rainbow at night! These are called moonbows, but they are very rare and difficult to photograph.

Rainbows also appear when the Sun shines through the drops of water spraying from a waterfall. This photo shows a rainbow at the Niagara Falls in North America.

Tell me why...
the sky roars and flashes

Thunder and lightning happen when a sudden burst of electricity escapes from tall storm clouds. This static electricity is created when water droplets and ice crystals are tossed up and down inside the clouds, by strong air currents, so that they rub against each other. Eventually, the built-up energy is released as a flash of lightning, which zigzags down to the ground or jumps between clouds. The sparks of lightning are so hot that they make the air suddenly spread out and shake at great speed, producing a loud crash of thunder.

Lightning jumps down to the ground and back up to the clouds again along the same path. If lightning strikes a tree, it can set it on fire.

Counting game
To find out how far away a storm is in kilometres, count the seconds between the lightning and the thunder and divide by 2.5. Lightning and thunder happen at the same time, but you see the lightning before you hear the thunder because light travels much faster than sound.

19

Tell me why...
the sky is blue

Sunlight is made up of lots of different colours of light. When it reaches the Earth's atmosphere, the different colours of light are scattered in all directions by gases and particles in the air. But the blue light is scattered more than the other colours because it travels a shorter distance. This means that, when you look at the sky on a clear day, you see more of the blue parts of light – and so the sky appears blue.

Black sky

Space looks black because there are no particles there to scatter the colours in sunlight. The sunlight travels in straight lines and we cannot see the colours that we see in the sky on Earth.

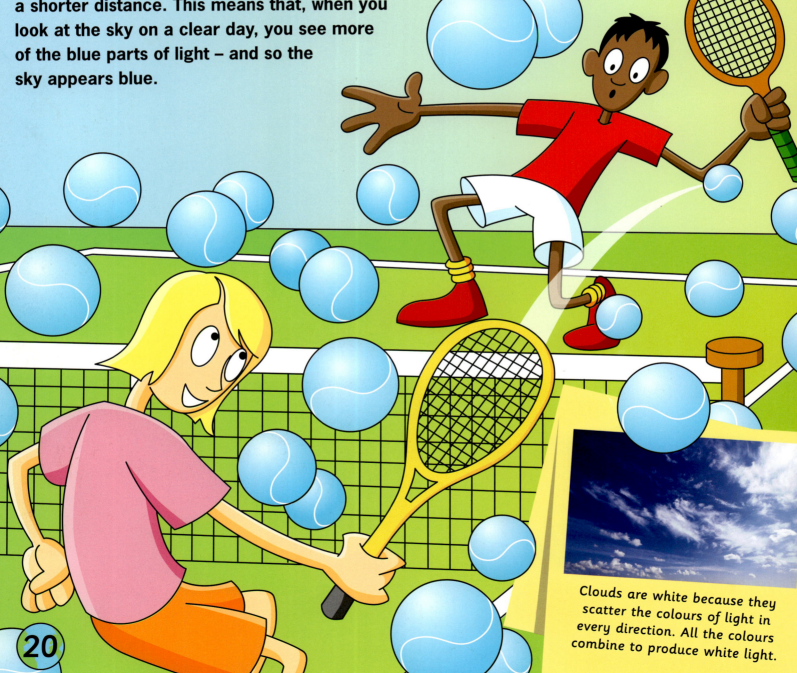

Clouds are white because they scatter the colours of light in every direction. All the colours combine to produce white light.

20

Tell me why...
sunsets are red

When the Sun begins to set, it is lower in the sky and its rays have to travel through more of the Earth's atmosphere before reaching you. More of the light bounces off particles in the air and is scattered. All the colours are scattered too far away from the Earth to be seen, except for red and orange. The red and orange colours are the only ones to reach your eyes, so the sky looks red as the Sun sets beneath the horizon.

Super sunsets

The tiny particles of dust and gas thrown high into the sky by volcanoes sometimes cause spectacular sunsets. The extra particles scatter most of the colours away and only the deep reds remain to reach your eyes.

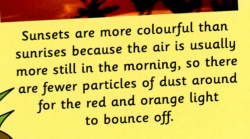

Sunsets are more colourful than sunrises because the air is usually more still in the morning, so there are fewer particles of dust around for the red and orange light to bounce off.

Tell me why...

the tide comes in and goes out

Tides are the way the sea moves up and down the beach every day. At high tide, the sea is near the top of the beach. At low tide the sea is near the bottom of the beach. There are usually two high tides and two low tides each day. Tides happen because the Moon and the Sun pull the Earth's oceans towards them with a force called gravity. The Moon's gravity is the main pulling force because it is much nearer to the Earth than the Sun is.

The difference between the high and low tides in Canada's Bay of Fundy is as much as 16 metres! This is because of the unique size and shape of the bay.

Spring tides

Spring tides are higher and lower than normal tides. They happen twice a month, when the Sun, Moon and Earth are all lined up. The pull of the Sun and the pull of the Moon combine to make a super-strong tugging force at these times.

23

Tell me why...
caves form underground

When rainwater drains down through the cracks in limestone rocks, it eats into the soft rocks, carving out big, underground rooms called caves. The rainwater contains acids, which break up the rocks into tiny pieces. These pieces of rock disappear into the water and are washed away in rivers that flow underground. Only a few millimetres of limestone are washed away in a year, so it can take thousands of years for large caves to form.

The incredible decorations inside Carlsbad Caverns, New Mexico, USA, make them look like wedding cakes! They formed when billions of drops of water deposited minerals they were carrying to form rocky icicles, pillars or domes.

Cave creatures

Many cave creatures, such as cave fish, are blind because their eyes are no use in the dark. They rely instead on their senses of touch and smell to find their way around and to locate food.

Tell me why...
some rocks contain crystals

Crystals grow inside rocks when the minerals that make up the rocks have enough space to grow into their natural geometric shape. This often happens when liquid rock from deep inside the Earth cools and hardens. Sometimes, heat and pressure underground concentrate minerals in pockets of rock or very hot water. Then the minerals cool to form crystals. Crystals can be cut and polished to form sparkling gemstones.

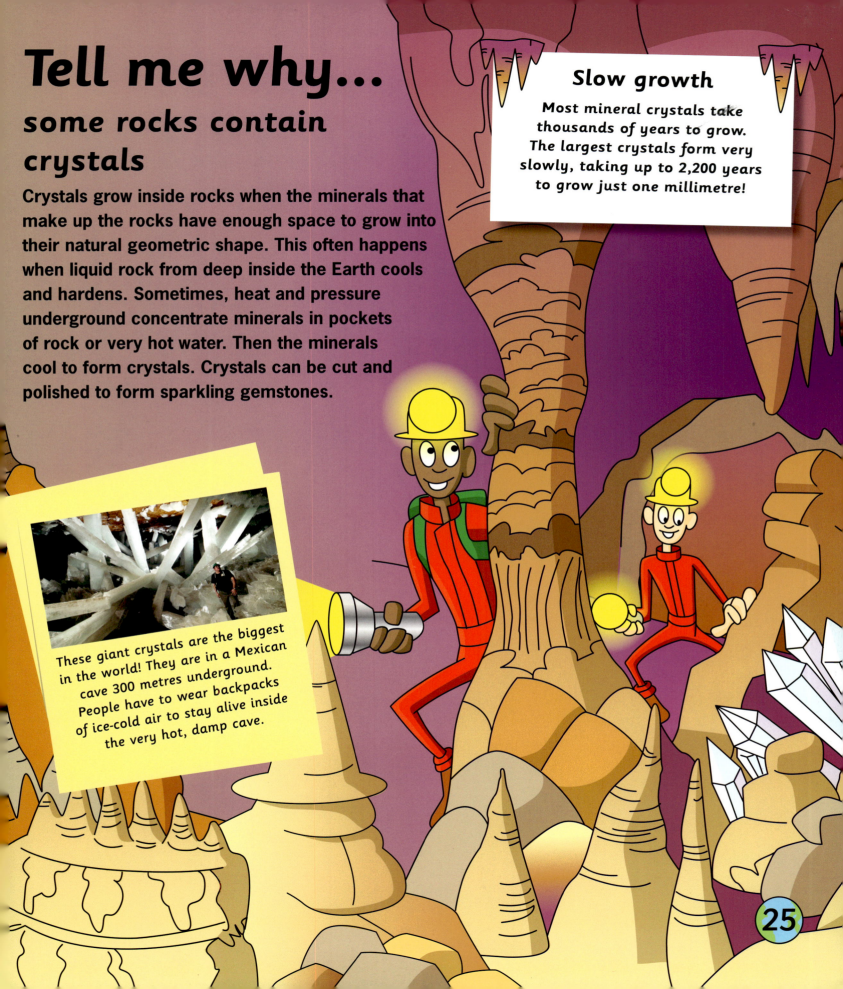

These giant crystals are the biggest in the world! They are in a Mexican cave 300 metres underground. People have to wear backpacks of ice-cold air to stay alive inside the very hot, damp cave.

Slow growth

Most mineral crystals take thousands of years to grow. The largest crystals form very slowly, taking up to 2,200 years to grow just one millimetre!

Tell me why...
dinosaurs are hiding in the rocks

Living dinosaurs are not really lurking in the rocks, waiting to jump out and surprise you! However, the remains of many dinosaurs that died millions of years ago are still trapped in the rocks of our planet. They are preserved as stone fossils. From dinosaur fossils, scientists can work out things such as how big they were, what they ate, how fast they moved, how they looked after their babies and even how they communicated with each other.

Dinosaur footprints, preserved in the rock, tell us how many toes dinosaurs had on their feet. This one was probably a meat-eater that walked on two legs.

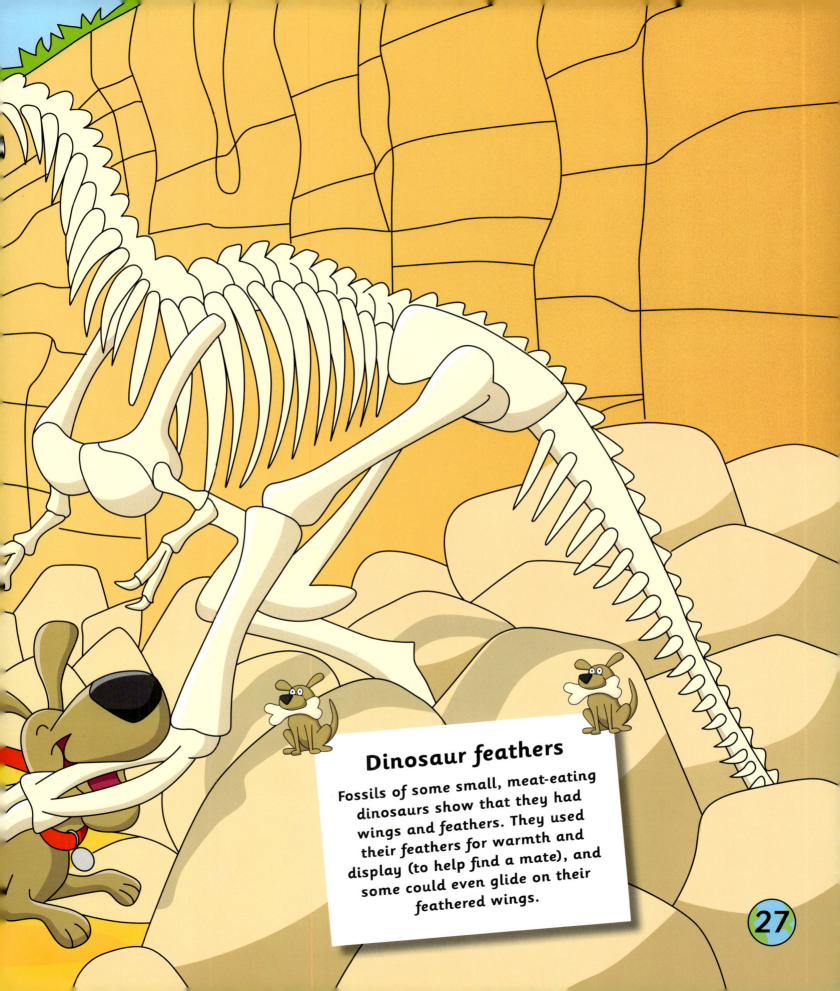

Dinosaur feathers

Fossils of some small, meat-eating dinosaurs show that they had wings and feathers. They used their feathers for warmth and display (to help find a mate), and some could even glide on their feathered wings.

Tell me why...
rainforests are like coral reefs

Rainforests and coral reefs are home to the greatest variety of living things on planet Earth. They are warm environments with plenty of food for animals to eat and lots of places for them to shelter and raise their young. The structure of rainforests and coral reefs depends on living things. Trees form the giant climbing frame that supports a rainforest, while a coral reef is supported by the empty skeletons of dead coral animals. Rainforests and coral reefs have both been growing on our planet for millions of years.

Superforests

Rainforests cover only six per cent of the Earth's surface, but they are home to more than half of all the different kinds of plants and animals on Earth. Sadly, an area of rainforest the size of a football pitch is being destroyed every second.

28

Coral reefs are home to about one-third of all the different kinds of fish in the world. The fish usually have very bright colours. Their bright patterns and markings help them to recognize other fish like themselves.

STOP

GO

29

Glossary

acid
A chemical substance that breaks rocks down to form new minerals. Rainwater contains some carbonic acid, which is a weak acid consisting of carbon dioxide dissolved in water.

atmosphere
A blanket of gases around a massive object such as a planet, held in place by the pull of the object's gravity.

continent
One of the seven large areas of land on Earth. The Earth's continents are: Africa, Antarctica, Asia, Australia, Europe, North America and South America.

continental drift
The way the continents slowly move about on the surface of the globe because of powerful forces deep inside the Earth.

coral reef
An underwater structure made up of the skeletons of dead animals called corals, with living corals growing on top.

crystal
A hard, glassy-looking object made of minerals. Crystals have smooth faces, straight edges and symmetrical corners.

cumulus cloud
A fluffy, white, cauliflower-shaped cloud that forms at low levels in good weather. This cloud is named after the Latin word for 'heap up', which is 'cumulo'.

cumulonimbus cloud
A tall thundercloud, with a flat, dark base. It brings heavy rain, thunder, lightning and hail storms.

earthquake
A shaking of the ground caused by sudden movements of the rocks deep underground. The biggest earthquakes are triggered by the movement of the Earth's plates.

fault line
A long crack in the rocks in the Earth's crust, where blocks of rock slip past each other.

fossil
The remains or traces of living things from the past, preserved in the rocks.

geometric shape
A three-dimensional shape with a regular, symmetrical structure. Crystals form in one of seven geometric shapes (such as cubic or hexagonal) according to the arrangement of the molecules (tiny particles) inside them.

gravity
An invisible force of attraction between objects. The gravity of massive objects, such as the Earth, is very strong. The Earth's gravity stops things on its surface from flying off into space by pulling them towards its centre.

hot spring
A place where hot water, full of minerals, bubbles to the surface. The water is heated by hot rocks under the ground.

limestone
A layered rock made mainly from the mineral calcite, which is the main ingredient in seashells. Some limestone rocks are made from the shells of ancient sea creatures; others are made from chemicals.

meteors
Tiny lumps of rock or ice falling from space towards Earth. Many meteors burn up in the Earth's atmosphere, but if they reach the surface they are called meteorites.

mineral
A hard, natural substance in the ground that makes up rocks.

planet
A large ball of rock, metal or gas that orbits (goes around) a star. The Earth is a planet that orbits the Sun, our nearest star.

polar lands
The frozen lands around the Earth's north and south poles. The polar lands at the top of the planet are called the Arctic, and the lands at the bottom of the planet are called the Antarctic.

rainforest
A thick forest with tall trees, which is warm and wet all year round. Rainforests grow around the Earth's middle, near its 'waist'.

reflection
The bouncing back of light from a surface.

seasons
Regular changes in the pattern of the weather throughout the year. Some places have four seasons (spring, summer, autumn and winter); other places have two seasons (summer and winter or wet and dry seasons).

senses
The physical abilities that animals use to find out about their surroundings. Animals often have five senses: sight, hearing, smell, touch and taste.

spring tide
A very high or a very low tide that happens twice each month.

static electricity
A form of electricity produced when certain materials are rubbed together. Lightning is a huge spark of static electricity.

stratus cloud
A very low-level, flat, shapeless cloud that can cover the whole sky. On the ground, stratus clouds form mist or fog. They often give long periods of rain.

tsunami
A giant sea wave caused by an underwater earthquake.

vent
An opening in the ground through which volcanic materials (such as hot, liquid rocks from deep underground) escape to the Earth's surface.

water vapour
The invisible gas that water turns into when it is heated.

Index

The Publisher would like to thank the following for permission to reproduce their material. Every care has been taken to trace copyright holders. However, if there have been unintentional omissions or failure to trace copyright holders, we apologize and will, if informed, endeavour to make corrections in any future edition.

Pages 4 Shutterstock/ixpert; 6 Shutterstock/marcokenya; 7 Corbis/Stephen Dalton; 9 Corbis/Frans Lanting; 10 Shutterstock/bierchen; 12 Shutterstock/axel2001; 13 Corbis/Roger Ressmeyer; 14 Science Photo Library/NOAA; 16 Shutterstock/Krill Smirnov; 17 Shutterstock/RZ-photo; 19 Shutterstock/Robert Fesus; 20 Shutterstock/Krill Smirnov; 21 Shutterstock/magdanatka; 22 Corbis/Richard Nowitz; 24 Corbis/Doug Meek; 25 Science Photo Library/Javier Trueba/MSF; 26 Shutterstock/kamuan; 29 Shutterstock/Vlad61.